MW01323869

SCRIPTURE NOVENAS

Novena of Hope in Suffering

Prepared by
the Daughters of St. Paul in Brazil

Translated from the Portuguese by
Germana Santos, FSP

BOOKS & MEDIA
Boston

Texts of the New Testament used in this work are taken from *The St. Paul Catholic Edition of the New Testament,* translated by Mark A. Wauck, copyright © 1992, Society of St. Paul. All rights reserved.

Texts of the Psalms used in this work are translated by Manuel Miguens, copyright © 1995, Daughters of St. Paul.

All other Old Testament scripture quotations are from the *New Revised Standard Version Bible, Catholic Edition,* copyright © 1993 and 1989 by the Division of Christian Education of the National Council of the Churches of Christ in the U.S.A. Used by permission. All rights reserved.

ISBN 0-8198-5147-7

Original Portuguese edition: Copyright © Pie Sociedade Filhas de São Paulo—SP.

Copyright © 2000, Daughters of St. Paul

Printed and published in the U.S.A. by Pauline Books & Media, 50 Saint Pauls Avenue, Boston MA 02130-3491.

www.pauline.org

Pauline Books & Media is the publishing house of the Daughters of St. Paul, an international congregation of women religious serving the Church with the communications media.

2 3 4 5 6 7 8   06 05 04 03 02 01

WHAT IS A NOVENA?

Most families have traditions—cherished customs and practices handed on from one generation to another. A novena is like that—a Catholic "family tradition," a type of prayer that is one of the ways our family of faith has prayed for centuries.

The Catholic tradition of praying novenas comes from the earliest days of the Church. After the ascension of Jesus, the Acts of the Apostles tells us that the Apostles and Mary gathered together and "devoted themselves single-mindedly to prayer" (Acts 1:14). And on the day of Pentecost, the Spirit of the Lord came to them. Based on this, Christians have always prayed for various needs, trusting that God both hears and answers prayer. Over time, the custom of praying for nine consecutive days for a particular need came to be called praying "a novena," since *novena* means *nine*.

There are many different kinds of novenas, but their purpose is the same: we call to mind our needs and we ask God's help and protection while remembering how much God loves us. And as we pray, we also ask for a greater understanding and acceptance of God's mysterious workings in our life and the lives of those we love.

"But," we might wonder, "doesn't God know our needs before we even ask; isn't praying once for something enough?" Although we believe in God's love for us, sometimes we need to remind ourselves of this. Although we know we are held in God's hands and that God will not let go, sometimes we need reassurance. In times of darkness, we need something to hold on to; in times of joy, we want to keep rejoicing! What may appear to be mere repetition in a novena is really a continual act of faith and hope in our loving God.

Like the rosary, the Stations of the Cross, the Liturgy of the Hours, or meal prayers, novenas are one small part of our Catholic faith. The greatest prayer of all is the Eucharistic Celebration. The Eucharist is central to Catholic living; from this great source flows the answer to all our human longings. Through praying with Scripture in this novena, may we draw near our Eucharistic God with confidence, "to receive mercy and find grace to help us in time of need" (Hebrews 4:16).

NOVENA OF HOPE
IN SUFFERING

lmost anytime we turn on the evening news, open a newspaper, or even chat with someone in a checkout line, we are likely to hear about suffering. Actually, we don't have to go any further than our own experience to realize that suffering is unavoidable, and that the way we live through moments of adversity often influences the rest of our lives.

No matter how much we want to avoid it, we cannot escape the simple fact that suffering happens in this world, and its reality is a mystery that Jesus himself lived through. By reflecting on Jesus' passion and death, we realize that the Father is close to those who suffer. The Father did not abandon Jesus, but was with him to the end and raised him in victory over death. Likewise, we are not alone in our darkness. In a mysterious yet very real way, we are companioned through our suffering; we are offered final victory over our darkness in the company of Jesus our Savior.

To be done on a daily basis

For nine consecutive days, set apart time for quiet reflection on the true meaning of your life. The title given to each day is the theme for that day. Try to center your meditation on the biblical thoughts suggested for the day in light of this theme, and bear in mind your own needs and desires.

Remind yourself that you are in God's presence. Ask God to bless you and all those you love as you hold in your heart the persons and intentions that you especially desire to pray for. Confidently express these intentions to God.

Pray the **Opening Prayer,** and then begin to meditate on the day's scripture passage. Allow a slow, peaceful repetition of the Word of

God to nourish whatever within you may be barren and dry, anxious and afraid. Try to open your heart to hear the Lord speaking to you about your situation. Pay attention to any unexpected thoughts or feelings that arise during your prayer…is God extending any invitations to you regarding your prayer intentions?

As you come to the end of your prayer time, spend some moments silently recalling the day's theme. End your prayer time by praying an **Our Father, Hail Mary, Glory Be,** and the **Closing Prayer.**

Opening Prayer
(for each day)

O God, your only Son Jesus gave us the ideal example of living and dying faithfully. Grant us the grace to live our lives as your children, and to face our daily dyings with hope and faith in your ever-present love. Through your Son, our Lord Jesus Christ, in the unity of the Holy Spirit, one God forever and ever. Amen.

Closing Prayer
(for each day)

We give you thanks, Lord God, because by your Son's death you destroyed our death. Through your grace, may we remember that you are with us in whatever sufferings we face in our life. Full of trust, may we live with the certain hope of being with you one day in glory. Through your Son, our Lord Jesus Christ, in the unity of the Holy Spirit, one God forever and ever. Amen.

WE ARE SAFE IN GOD'S KEEPING

Opening prayer *(page 11)*

For meditation

> He said, "Do not fear, greatly beloved, you are safe. Be strong and courageous!" When he spoke to me, I was strengthened and said, "Let my Lord speak, for you have strengthened me."
>
> Daniel 10:19

> Protect me, O God,
>   for in you I take refuge.
> I say to the Lord,
>   "You are my Lord;
> I have no good apart from you."
>
> Psalm 16:1–2

To recall throughout the day

*Why are you cast down, O my soul,
    and why are you disquieted within me?
Hope in God; for I shall again praise him,
    my help and my God.*

Psalm 42:5–6

Closing prayer (page 12)

THE DEATH OF THE JUST ONE

Opening prayer *(page 11)*

For meditation

The righteous man will thrive
   like a palm tree,
will grow like a cedar on Mount Lebanon;
planted in the house of the Lord,
they will thrive in the courts of our God.

Psalm 92:13–14

There were some who pleased God
   and were loved by him,
and while living among sinners were
   taken up.
They were caught up so that evil

might not change their understanding
   or guile deceive their souls.
For the fascination of wickedness
   obscures what is good,
and roving desire perverts the innocent mind.
Being perfected in a short time,
   they fulfilled long years;
for their souls were pleasing to the Lord,
therefore he took them quickly from
   the midst of wickedness.

Wisdom 4:10–14

To recall throughout the day

*Why are you cast down, O my soul,
   and why are you disquieted within me?
Hope in God; for I shall again praise him,
   my help and my God.*

Psalm 42:5–6

Closing prayer (page 12)

THOSE WHO DIE ARE WITH CHRIST

Opening prayer (page 11)

For meditation

"Let not your hearts be troubled!
Believe in God and believe in me.
In my Father's house are many rooms;
were it not so, would I have told you
   that I am going to prepare a place for you?
And if I go and prepare a place for you,
   I will come again and take you to myself,
so that where I am, you too may be."

John 14:1–3

Brothers, we want you to understand how it is with those who have fallen asleep, so you will not grieve like others do, who have no hope. For if we believe that Jesus died and rose again, then through Jesus God will also bring with him those who have fallen asleep. Encourage one another with these words.

1 Thessalonians 4:13–14, 18

To recall throughout the day

*Why are you cast down, O my soul,
    and why are you disquieted within me?
Hope in God; for I shall again praise him,
    my help and my God.*

Psalm 42:5–6

Closing prayer *(page 12)*

GOD IS EVER PRESENT

Opening prayer *(page 11)*

For meditation

Then I heard a loud voice from the throne say, "Behold, God's dwelling is now with men. He shall dwell with them and they shall be his people, and God himself will be with them. He will wipe every tear from their eyes and death shall be no more—no more grief or crying or pain, for what came before has passed away."

Then the One seated on the throne said: "Behold, I will make all things new!"

He also said: "Write this down, for these words are trustworthy and true." Then he said to me, "It is finished! I am the Alpha and the

Omega, the beginning and the end. Those who thirst I will allow to drink freely from the spring of living water. Whoever is victorious shall inherit all these things, and I shall be his God and he shall be my son."

Revelation 21:3–7

To recall throughout the day

Why are you cast down, O my soul,
  and why are you disquieted within me?
Hope in God; for I shall again praise him,
  my help and my God.

Psalm 42:5–6

Closing prayer (page 12)

Jesus' Own Suffering Gives Us Hope

Opening prayer (page 11)

For meditation

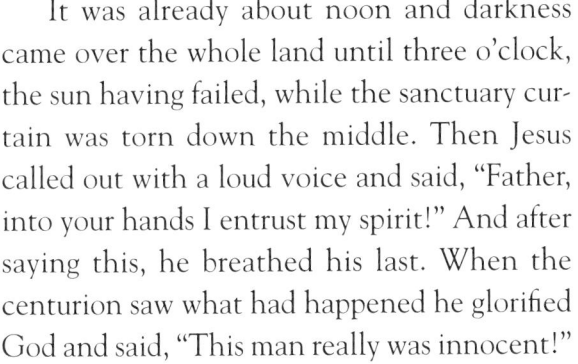

It was already about noon and darkness came over the whole land until three o'clock, the sun having failed, while the sanctuary curtain was torn down the middle. Then Jesus called out with a loud voice and said, "Father, into your hands I entrust my spirit!" And after saying this, he breathed his last. When the centurion saw what had happened he glorified God and said, "This man really was innocent!"

Luke 23:44–47

For the sake of the joy that lay before him he endured the cross and thought nothing of the shame of it, and is now seated at the right hand of God's throne. Think of Jesus, who endured so much hostility from sinners, and do not let your souls grow weary or lose your courage.

Hebrews 12:2–3

To recall throughout the day

Why are you cast down, O my soul,
and why are you disquieted within me?
Hope in God; for I shall again praise him,
my help and my God.

Psalm 42:5–6

Closing prayer (page 12)

JESUS IS ALIVE

Opening prayer *(page 11)*

For meditation

But on the first day of the week, at early dawn, the women came to the tomb bringing the aromatic spices they had prepared. They found the stone rolled away from the tomb and when they went in they did not find the Lord Jesus' body, and it happened that when they were at a loss over this, behold, two men in dazzling clothes stood near them. The women were terrified and bowed their faces to the ground, and the men said to them, "Why are you looking for he who lives among the dead? He is not here—he is risen."

Luke 24:1–6

[Jesus] also provided them with many proofs that he was still alive after his sufferings; for a period of forty days he appeared to them and spoke to them about the Kingdom of God.

Acts 1:3

To recall throughout the day

Why are you cast down, O my soul,
  and why are you disquieted within me?
Hope in God; for I shall again praise him,
  my help and my God.

Psalm 42:5–6

Closing prayer (page 12)

WITH CHRIST WE CONQUER DEATH

Opening prayer *(page 11)*

For meditation

But if we have died with Christ we believe that we will also come to life with him, for we know that Christ rose from the dead and will never die again—death no longer has any power over him. For the death he died he died to sin once and for all, and the life he lives he lives for God.

Romans 6:8–10

For if we believe that Jesus died and rose again, then through Jesus God will also bring with him those who have fallen asleep.

1 Thessalonians 4:14

To recall throughout the day

Why are you cast down, O my soul,
  and why are you disquieted within me?
Hope in God; for I shall again praise him,
  my help and my God.

Psalm 42:5–6

Closing prayer (page 12)

IN EVERYTHING, WE BELONG TO GOD

Opening prayer (page 11)

For meditation

"I am praying for them;
I am praying, not for the world,
   but for those you have given me,
because they are yours and everything
   of mine is yours and yours is mine,
and I am glorified in them."

John 17:9–10

We none of us live for ourselves and we none of us die for ourselves, for if we live we live for the Lord and if we die we die for the

Lord. And so whether we live or whether we die we belong to the Lord. This is why Christ died and came to life—so he would be Lord of both the dead and the living.

Romans 14:7–9

To recall throughout the day

Why are you cast down, O my soul,
  and why are you disquieted within me?
Hope in God; for I shall again praise him,
  my help and my God.

Psalm 42:5–6

Closing prayer (page 12)

WE HAVE THE ASSURANCE OF LIFE

Opening prayer *(page 11)*

For meditation

"Now this is the will of him who sent me
that I should lose nothing of what
   he gave me,
but should raise it up on the last day.
For this is the will of my Father,
that everyone who sees the Son
   and believes
in him should have eternal life,
and I will raise him up on the last day."

John 6:39–40

Blessed be the God and Father of our Lord Jesus Christ! In his great mercy we have been reborn to a living hope through the resurrection of Jesus Christ from the dead and to an imperishable, undefiled, and unfading inheritance, which is reserved in Heaven for you who by God's power are guarded through faith for the salvation which is ready to be revealed in the last days.

1 Peter 1:3–5

To recall throughout the day

Why are you cast down, O my soul,
  and why are you disquieted within me?
Hope in God; for I shall again praise him,
  my help and my God.

Psalm 42:5–6

Closing prayer *(page 12)*

Titles in the series of *Scripture Novenas:*

#0-8198-5140-X   Novena for Health

#0-8198-5141-8   Novena for Families

#0-8198-5142-6   Novena in a Time of Difficulty

#0-8198-5143-4   Novena in Praise of the Father

#0-8198-5144-2   Novena in Praise of the Son

#0-8198-5145-0   Novena in Praise of the Holy Spirit

#0-8198-5146-9   Novena of Forgiveness

#0-8198-5147-7   Novena of Hope in Suffering

#0-8198-5148-5   Novena of Thanksgiving

#0-8198-5149-3   Novena to Find Employment

#0-8198-5150-7   Novena to Obtain Patience

#0-8198-5151-5   Novena to Overcome Fear

Pauline BOOKS & MEDIA

The Daughters of St. Paul operate book and media centers at the following addresses. Visit, call or write the one nearest you today, or find us on the World Wide Web, www.pauline.org

CALIFORNIA
3908 Sepulveda Blvd, Culver City, CA 90230   310-397-8676
5945 Balboa Avenue, San Diego, CA 92111   858-565-9181
46 Geary Street, San Francisco, CA 94108   415-781-5180

FLORIDA
145 S.W. 107th Avenue, Miami, FL 33174   305-559-6715

HAWAII
1143 Bishop Street, Honolulu, HI 96813   808-521-2731
Neighbor Islands call: 800-259-8463

ILLINOIS
172 North Michigan Avenue, Chicago, IL 60601   312-346-4228

LOUISIANA
4403 Veterans Memorial Blvd, Metairie, LA 70006   504-887-7631

MASSACHUSETTS
Rte. 1, 885 Providence Hwy, Dedham, MA 02026   781-326-5385

MISSOURI
9804 Watson Road, St. Louis, MO 63126   314-965-3512

NEW JERSEY
561 U.S. Route 1, Wick Plaza, Edison, NJ 08817   732-572-1200

NEW YORK
150 East 52nd Street, New York, NY 10022   212-754-1110
78 Fort Place, Staten Island, NY 10301   718-447-5071

OHIO
2105 Ontario Street, Cleveland, OH 44115   216-621-9427

PENNSYLVANIA
9171-A Roosevelt Blvd, Philadelphia PA 19114   215-676-9494

SOUTH CAROLINA
243 King Street, Charleston, SC 29401   843-577-0175

TENNESSEE
4811 Poplar Avenue, Memphis, TN 38117   901-761-2987

TEXAS
114 Main Plaza, San Antonio, TX 78205   210-224-8101

VIRGINIA
1025 King Street, Alexandria, VA 22314   703-549-3806

CANADA
3022 Dufferin Street, Toronto, Ontario, Canada M6B 3T5   416-781-9131
1155 Yonge Street, Toronto, Ontario, Canada M4T 1W2   416-934-3440

¡También somos su fuente para libros, videos y música en español!